*After years of research and countless hours of studying political history, it has been determined that policies viciously executed with the stroke of a pen during a single presidency, gave us many reasons to vote for Republicans.

I0408279

*See Cover

B

BAR

BARA

BARAC

BARACK

BARACK O

BARACK OB

BARACK OBA

BARACK OBAM

BARACK OBAMA

BARACK OBAMA

BARACK OBAMA

BARACK OBAMA

BARACK OBAMA

BARACK OBAMA

BARACK OBAMA

BARACK OBAMA

BARACK OBAMA

BARACK OBAMA

BARACK OBAMA

BARACK OBAMA

*The president who shares the same number as this page.

*See Cover

*See Cover

B

BAR

BARA

BARAC

BARACK

BARACK O

BARACK OB

BARACK OBA

BARACK OBAM

BARACK OBAMA

BARACK OBAMA

BARACK OBAMA

BARACK OBAMA

BARACK OBAMA

BARACK OBAMA

BARACK OBAMA

BARACK OBAMA

BARACK OBAMA

BARACK OBAMA

BARACK OBAMA

*See Cover

*See Cover

*See Cover

B

BARA

BARAC

BARACK

BARACK O

BARACK OB

BARACK OBA

BARACK OBAM

BARACK OBAMA

BARACK OBAMA

BARACK OBAMA

BARACK OBAMA

BARACK OBAMA

BARACK OBAMA

BARACK OBAMA

BARACK OBAMA

BARACK OBAMA

BARACK OBAMA

BARACK OBAMA

BARACK OBAMA

B

BARA

BARAC

BARACK

BARACK O

BARACK OB

BARACK OBA

BARACK OBAM

BARACK OBAMA

BARACK OBAMA

BARACK OBAMA

BARACK OBAMA

BARACK OBAMA

BARACK OBAMA

BARACK OBAMA

BARACK OBAMA

BARACK OBAMA

BARACK OBAMA

BARACK OBAMA

BARACK OBAMA

BARACK OBAMA

BARACK OBAMA

BARACK OBAMA

BARACK OBAMA

BARACK OBAMA

BARACK OBAMA

BARACK OBAMA

BARACK OBAMA

BARACK OBAMA

BARACK OBAMA

BARACK OBAMA

BARACK OBAMA

BARACK OBAMA

BARACK OBAMA

BARACK OBAMA

BARACK OBAMA

Author's Note

I am in no way authorized to tell you who you should vote for. I can only plead my case as to *how* you should vote. I believe you should stick to your values and vote your conscious.

When I went to college to earn my bachelor's degree in Journalism, I was told repeatedly *what* I should think. I was told what specific articles to research. I was never given the option of *how* to think. You see, I'm a moderate conservative. I have voted Republican on every ballot since I could vote. I fought leftist ideas from most of my professors and fortunately, made it through college. I continue to challenge those ideas in the workplace, as you can imagine most newsrooms these days are filled with people who despise conservative values.

So now you may be wondering why I decided to write a book that contradicts how I feel about people telling you who to vote for and suggests you should vote for Republicans. The answer: *money. Bernie Sanders was right* when he spoke to voters about the rising cost of tuition. America is facing a debt crisis and the system is rigged in such a way that it makes it impossible to land a solid job in your career field without a college education. Without gaining massive amounts of student loan debt, your dream job is almost unreachable. I have so much student loan debt and I'm tired of it. I want it gone. So, I want to thank you for buying my book and I hope it has brought a smile to your face.

Hopefully, this will spark a conversation so that our democracy continues to be robust in discussion on policy and the American values that make this country great. So great, in fact, that it enables someone like myself to make money on a book filled with blank pages.

Proud Capitalist,

Eric Sykes